IS TAX THEFT? UNEARTHINGTHE PSYCHOLOGY BEHIND COMMISSION OF TAX FRAUD

VOLUME 2, ISSUE 3 OF BRILLOPEDIA

TUSHTI RATNAPRIYA THAKUR AND SWARNIKA

Contents

Preface

"Start writing, no matter what. The water does not flow until the faucet is turned on".

- Louis L'Amour

Hundreds of students and professors are contributing their work to Brillopedia, we are here to provide ample information about Law and Contemporary issues. Our aim is to provide a platform for today's generation to express their views and ideas on law and contemporary law.

Authors

CHAPTER ONE

ABSTRACT

The development of any economy demands an inflow of cash which is to be utilized for the conduct of various activities that would contribute to its growth. Raw materials, their processing, labour force and possibly all developmental tasks require monetary funding. Further, the very administration and governance of a country would also be virtually defunct if not met with necessary financial assistance. This system of providing the governing bodies with necessary funding to ensure the upliftment and stability has been present in the society since times immemorial whilst being cloaked under the shadow of one form or the other. This primeval system, however, has undergone a plethora of changes which has culminated in a complex apparatus of laws and methods to evade those laws. This paper attempts at understanding foremostly, the mandate behind the compulsion of paying taxes and secondly, the psyche behind the attempts at escaping this duty or "liability". An attempt would be made to outline the divergence between the importance of paying tax and the mob mentality of evading this responsibility.

<u>KEYWORDS</u>: Tax evasion, tax fraud, tax avoidance, compulsory charge, liability, canons of taxation, public order

INTRODUCTION

THE GENESIS OF TAXATION IN INDIA

The germination of the system of taxation can be referenced far back to the ancient times as traced under the writings of Manusmriti and Arthasastra. According to the Sastras, Manu, the ancient scholar and lawgiver, said that it is proper for the king to impose taxes. His philosophy was inclined towards the determination of taxes by taking into consideration both the expenses and earnings of the subjects of the kingdom. However, he warned the king against collecting excessively in taxes and said that he should stray away from the poles of excessive or utter absence of taxing. It was suggested that the king should set up tax collecting such that the people paying the taxes do not experience financial hardship, where the payments could be flexibly made in the form of grains, raw materials, gold-coins and rendering of services. Moreover, the two-fold distinction between direct and indirect taxes which has continued its existence up to the modern times can also be found in the ramages of this ancient system.

Fast-forwarding to the modern era, the codification of taxation and its subsequent translation into statutory laws contained in the Acts was sprouted during the British regime, owing to the financial difficulties that culminated after the mutiny of 1857. With the first legislation laying its foundation in the year 1860, the tax laws continued to extend their arms into new promulgations in the coming years of 1886, 1918, 1922 and finally, climaxed with the passing of the current governing legislation - the Income Tax Act, 1961. Owing to the recurring changes in and complexity of the financial system, this Act has undergone several amendments over the years and is supported by the Income Tax Rules of 1962 for its implementation. The rapid changes in the execution and administration of taxes is reflective of the saga of socio-economic thinking in India. However, through the series of changes, the objective of the taxation system has nevertheless remained the same and is essentially subsumed under two very broad categories of economic development and welfare functions that the government is charged with performing. Elaboratively, the government's imposition of tax is crucial for meeting the following functions :

1. Maintenance of public order
2. Military expenditures
3. Enforcement of public order and law
4. Protection and development of public property, economic infrastructure including construction of roads, enforcement of contracts and legal tenders public works
5. Social engineering which involves the utilisation of planned development for the management of a society's progress and its citizens
6. Providing fund for welfare and public services including aid to education and healthcare systems, unemployment benefits
7. Pensions for the elderly
8. Provisions for energy, water and waste management systems, common public utilities and public transportation

Hence, at the crux of tax collection rests the discharge of essential functions by the government for the maintenance of the society and its economic stability. While the government can also rely on other channels of financial funding such as sale of public assets, these are not recurring activities and hence a dynamic and an everlasting system such as taxation is necessary for the very operation of the government itself as even administrators are also paid through the revenue that the State collects from its subjects.

CHAPTER THREE

TAX EVASION VS TAX AVOIDANCE: THE ESCAPE PSYCHOLOGY

The core principles of taxation as envisaged by Adam Smith have remained largely unchanged even after two centuries. These principles advocate that a good system of taxation rests on certain fundamental canons that promote equity, certainty and convenience, where the administration cost of tax collection is considerably lowered for the public. This leads us to the question that if the principles and functions of taxes are considerably aimed at public benefit, why is it that the general public mentality is more inclined towards escaping this responsibility that is for their own good? This can be answered by glancing at the following definitions of taxation :

1. According to Bastable, "A tax is a compulsory contribution of the wealth of a person, or body of persons for the service of public powers."
2. According to Hugh Dalton, "A tax is a compulsory charge imposed by a public authority irrespective of the exact amount of service rendered to the taxpayer in return and not imposed as a penalty for legal offense."
3. According to Trussing, "The essence of tax as distinguished from other charges by the government is the absence of direct quid pro quo- tit for tat between the taxpayers and the public authority."

Thus, from the above-mentioned definitions what can be inferred is that - Firstly, payment of taxes is independent of the will of the party as it is compulsory in nature. Secondly, tax is levied by the government to enable itself to provide necessary services to its citizens. Finally and most importantly, that there is no quid-pro-quo between the taxpayers and the public authority levying the tax, which implies that paying taxes does not entitle taxpayers to any services distinguishable from those who do not pay taxes. Since, the human mind works on an undeniable correlation between effort and rewards, a lack of any special advantages for the taxpayers and the utilisation of their hard earned tax money for the welfare of the public in general, regardless of whether and how much tax one pays, can be rightly deduced to be a significant demotivator that pushes the taxpayers away from their duty towards the nation and towards commission of tax fraud.

It is with relation to the term "tax fraud" that it becomes important to distinguish tax evasion from its look-alike tax avoidance. While both tax evasion and tax avoidance cause hefty losses in tax revenue, shifting the burden to handful abiding citizens, there is a markedly significant difference between the two, that is, their legality. Tax avoidance, while being immoral, is not an illegality in the eyes of law, but rather a smart curation of loopholes that exist in the system for one's benefit. Typically, this is done by utilising all permitted deductions and credits. It can also be done by giving tax-beneficial investments a higher priority, such as purchasing tax-free municipal bonds. Therefore, it plays on the technicalities of tax laws to avoid responsibility of its payments. However, tax evasion is both immoral and illegal, and constitutes a prima facie infringement of taxation laws utilising techniques such as inflating one's expenses by charging personal expenses as costs incurred while transacting business, manipulation of accounts to show reduced income, unrecorded sales, presenting bogus receipts of charitable donations to avoid liability under Section 8G of the Act and non-disclosure of income from benami transactions.

Further, an elaborate discussion of the points of distinction between the tax evasion and the employment of legal strategies to reduce an individual's or a company's income tax liability known as tax avoidance leads us to draw the following conclusions:

- Tax evasion, which relies on unethical practices like fabricating deductions and underreporting income, is not the same as tax avoidance.
- Tax avoidance is the adoption of any lawful strategy by a taxpayer to reduce the amount of income tax due.
- Tax avoidance strategies can be used by both individual taxpayers and businesses to pay less in taxes.

- Tax avoidance includes using tax deductions, credits, income exclusions, and loopholes.
- These are authorised tax reductions that are provided to promote specific actions, like property ownership or retirement savings.
- Tax avoidance differs from tax evasion, which relies on unethical practices such as underreporting income.

In addition to a lack of distinction between the taxpayers and non-taxpayers by the government, a significant motivation behind tax evasion is shadowed behind the "canon of equity" which provides that the amount of tax one has to pay is directly proportional to their income. Therefore, significant proportions of salaries have to be paid as taxes, ranging to lacs and crores in some cases, a number so huge that people consciously refrain from this duty. Further, a lack of transparency in the government's spending of tax money does not help the cause and pushes its citizens to consider whether paying their taxes is actually a duty or a compulsory "theft" by the authorities.

CHAPTER FOUR

UNDERSTANDING TAX AVOIDANCE

Many people have access to lawful means of avoiding taxes or at the very least reducing their tax obligations. In fact, to reduce their lawful and legitimate tax debt to the Internal Revenue Service (IRS), millions of people and corporations employ various tax avoidance strategies.

Taxpayers may benefit from tax avoidance by utilising a number of credits, deductions, exclusions, and loopholes, including:

- making a child tax credit claim
- investing in retirement accounts and contributing the maximum amount possible each year
- claiming a tax deduction for a mortgage
- the act of funding a health savings account (HSA)

In order to efficiently perform tax planning, a taxpayer can make the most of various provisions of the Income Tax Act of 1961 by taking deductions under Sections 10, 80C, and 80U, as well as Sections 37 and others. On the other side, one example of efficient tax avoidance is a corporation moving its intellectual property to a nation with lower tax rates than India.The revenue of many countries, including India, is greatly reduced by the tax dodging tactics employed by large corporations worldwide. The government of India was obliged to rewrite its laws and treaties with other nations in response to the numerous incidents of tax avoidance that emerged over the past 20 years, some of which have been covered in length above. Through the Income Tax Act of 1961 and the Finance Act of 2015, the Indian Government established a number of regulations and guidelines to control and prevent tax evasion.The General

Anti-Avoidance Rule (GAAR) was a part of the 1961 Income Tax Act's Chapter X-A. GAAR was added to the Income Tax Act by the Finance Act of 2012, but it became effective on April 1st, 2017. A clause called "Section 96. Impermissible avoidance arrangement" was incorporated into the Income Tax Act with the sole intent of reducing tax avoidance tactics. The clause prohibited agreements or deals that were formed in order to receive a tax benefit.In order to replace a new corporate residency test that stated that a foreign company would be a tax resident of India if its place of effective management (POEM) was determined to be located in India, section 6(3) of the Finance Act, 2015 was amended. Prior to this change, a corporation that was not a resident of India was only considered a resident for tax purposes if it was controlled and managed there.The Indian government took a number of actions in 2017 to align rules and regulations with the Base Erosion and Profit Shifting (BEPS) recommendations made by the Organization for Economic Co-operation and Development (OECD), which could reduce the threat of tax evasion. These actions included BEPS action plans 13, 1, and 5. Although the large corporations use tax avoidance strategies to save billions of dollars annually, doing so costs the government a lot of money and creates an unfair market because an individual earning a salary or operating a small business has little knowledge or intelligence to develop tax avoidance strategies and ultimately pays their taxes in full. While large corporations continue to reduce their tax obligations through tax evasion. Since they manage to do it within the confines of the law, it is challenging to demonstrate that these corporate goliaths did in fact escape taxes. In truth, the success of these large corporations depends on how well they can minimise their tax liabilities while generating big returns for their investors. The principle underpinning tax avoidance still holds true: in addition to the transaction or agreement, the business must turn a healthy profit and avoid losing a sizable portion of that profit to taxes.In order to meet the demands of these businesses, which in turn aid in the development of these nations, numerous governments have reduced their tax rates. As a result, this particular nexus effectively aids in the avoidance of billions of Rupees in taxes, benefiting huge business houses from tax evasion.

CHAPTER FIVE

TAX FRAUD :PUBLIC VS. GOVERNMENT PERSPECTIVE

Why should I pay taxes, some people wonder. They contend: I have to pay for my food, my residence, my transportation, my medical care, and having a vehicle, which includes not only the cost of the vehicle but also vehicle taxes and other expenses. Further, one must pay toll taxes even on several roads. Additionally, they claim that when compared to nations like the USA and the UK, individuals in those nations receive social security and medical care essentially for nothing. India, however, does not provide such amenities. The fundamental premise of the field of economics known as "public choice" is that people in democracies perceive a relationship between the taxes they pay and the services they receive from the government. In other words, whether or not they believe their own tax burden is excessive, citizens elect governments to provide them with goods and services, and there is a sense in which every citizen must be aware that taxes must be paid to fnance public services. It indicates that every citizen is aware that if taxes are decreased, public services would also be lowered. A tax payer's overall perception of taxes as a burden leads them to try to minimise their tax liability or avoid paying them altogether. The tax rates were likewise astronomical in past years. Income tax rates reached as high as 97.75% inclusive of surcharge before the 1980s. But things are quickly shifting right now. Despite the fact that tax rates have been reduced, our country still does not have the same sophisticated tax culture. "Taxes are the price for civilisation," stated Justice Homes of the US Supreme Court. It's about time taxes were seen as a cost of civilisation rather than a burden. It is true that India does not give social security or free healthcare as several affluent nations do. But we must consider the problem on a wider scale. We must recognise that the government must fulfill a number of obligations, including providing health care through government hospitals (which often provide services at no cost), educating the public, and more (In Municipal and Government schools the fee is negligible). Additionally, the government offers cooking gas at a discounted price or provides subsidies. Of course, the government must spend the majority of its money on things like infrastructure improvements and national defence. The government uses taxes to fund a variety of welfare programmes, including job initiatives.The government must pay the administrative costs for the thousands of staff in the numerous departments. Even though the legal system is slow, the government is nevertheless required to provide the salaries and benefits of judges, magistrates, and other court employees. We must recognise that we must pay taxes in accordance with the law after taking into account these many governmental responsibilities. We must conduct ourselves as good citizens.The lack of a tax culture in India is a well-known reality. Despite significant attempts to broaden the tax base, our country still only has roughly 82.7 million taxpayers, or 6.25 percent of its more than 132 crore population, which is too few for it. On the other hand, in the United States, just roughly 45% of people pay taxes. There are a lot of causes behind this. Many Indians do not make enough money annually to even be required to pay income tax, but a bigger contributing cause is the absence of a tax culture as well as India's huge rural and underground economies.

CHAPTER SIX

CONCLUSION

The intricacies with which the law of taxation has been developed can be evidenced by how only a few professionals fully understand its working and are nevertheless prone to committing errors. Therefore, the pressing priority when it comes to promoting the citizens to rightfully pay the taxes due is to be focused towards simplification of tax laws and a concurrent reduction in tax rate by the government. Further, the ambiguity behind the government spendings of the tax money needs to be removed so that every citizen has a drone-like view of a system that is equitable, righteous and corruption free. Those who receive taxable income must declare it, pay the appropriate taxes, and file their income tax returns by the deadline. Interest and penalties may be assessed for failure to meet an obligation on time or in default. The authorities have the right to bring charges against guilty parties in some instances of tax evasion and other major mistakes. The department may conduct an investigation. Additionally, it includes a division called Investigations that has the authority to conduct searches and seizures. Therefore, extreme caution is required.